D0604513

# PLANTS

# THE KINGDOMS OF LIFE

# PLANTS

## Dr. Alvin, Virginia, and Robert Silverstein

## TWENTY-FIRST CENTURY BOOKS

A Division of Henry Holt and Company
New York

Twenty-First Century Books
A Division of Henry Holt and Company, Inc.
115 West 18th Street
New York, NY 10011

Henry Holt® and colophon are trademarks of
Henry Holt and Company, Inc.
*Publishers since 1866*

Published in Canada by Fitzhenry & Whiteside Ltd.
195 Allstate Parkway, Markham, Ontario L3R 4T8

**Library of Congress Cataloging-in-Publication Data**
Silverstein, Alvin.
Plants / Alvin Silverstein, Virginia Silverstein, and Robert Silverstein.—1st ed.
p. cm.—(The Kingdoms of life)
Includes index.
Summary: Begins with a general description of the plant kingdom and its classification
before going on to discuss specific kinds of plants.
1. Plants—Juvenile literature. 2. Botany—Juvenile literature. [1. Plants. 2. Botany.] I. Silverstein, Virginia B.
II. Silverstein, Robert A. III. Title. IV. Series: Silverstein, Alvin. The Kingdoms of life.
QK49.S54 1996                                                                            95-45673
581—dc20                                                                                        CIP
                                                                                                        AC

ISBN 0–8050–3519–2
First Edition 1996

*Designed by Kelly Soong*

Printed in the United States of America
All first editions are printed on acid-free paper ∞.
10 9 8 7 6 5 4 3 2 1

**Photo credits**

Cover: Stephen J. Krasemann/Photo Researchers, Inc.

p. 6 (clockwise from top right): Dave B. Fleetham/Tom Stack & Associates; Rod Planck/Tom Stack & Associates; Cabisco/Visuals Unlimited; M. I. Walker/Photo Researchers, Inc.; Zig Leszczynski/Earth Scenes; Bill Gause/Photo Researchers, Inc.; pp. 7, 35 (left), 47 (bottom): Zig Leszczynski; p. 8: Jeff Greenberg/Photo Researchers, Inc.; p. 10: Photo Researchers, Inc.; p. 11: Leonard Lee Rue Jr./Earth Scenes; p. 12: John Gerlach/Tom Stack & Associates; p. 13: Bob Pool/Tom Stack & Associates; pp. 17 (both), 43, 49: John Shaw/Tom Stack & Associates; p. 18: Doug Wechsler/Earth Scenes; p. 21: Gerald & Buff Corsi/Tom Stack & Associates; pp. 22, 33 (bottom): David M. Dennis/Tom Stack & Associates; p. 23 (top): Biophoto Associates/Photo Researchers, Inc.; p. 23 (bottom): Michael Fogden/Earth Scenes; pp. 25 (left), 34: Patti Murray/Earth Scenes; p. 25 (right): Richard Shiell/Earth Scenes; p. 26: Nancy Adams/Tom Stack & Associates; p.27: Joyce Photographics/Photo Researchers, Inc.; p. 27 (right): Michael P. Gadomski/Photo Researchers, Inc.; p. 28: D. Wilder/Tom Stack & Associates; p. 29: R. Ashley/Visuals Unlimited; pp. 30, 33 (top): E. R. Degginger/Earth Scenes; p. 31 (top): Robert P. Comport/Earth Scenes; pp. 31 (bottom), 39: Inga Spence/Tom Stack & Associates; p. 35 (right): G. Büttner/Naturbild/OKAPIA/Photo Researchers, Inc.; p. 36: Byron Augustin/Tom Stack & Associates: p. 37: Kjell B. Sandved/Visuals Unlimited; p. 40: John Kaprielian/Photo Researchers, Inc.; p. 41: Kenneth W. Fink/Photo Researchers, Inc.; p. 42: G. C. Kelley/Tom Stack & Associates: p. 44: Bertram G. Murray Jr./Earth Scenes; p. 45: Dr. Nigel Smith/Earth Scenes; p. 47 (top): Doug Sokell/Tom Stack & Associates; p. 48: Bob McKeever/Tom Stack & Associates; p. 50: Jack Dermid/Oxford Scientific Films/Earth Scenes; p. 52: Carson Baldwin Jr./Earth Scenes; p. 55: J. Alcock/Visuals Unlimited.

# CONTENTS

# THE KINGDOMS OF LIFE

## ANIMALS

Great horned owl

Day octopus

**VERTEBRATES**

**INVERTEBRATES**

## PLANTS

## FUNGI

Silver vase

Hygrophorus mushroom

## MONERANS

## PROTISTS

Cyanobacteria

Diatoms

# PLANTS

# 1

## OUR LIVING WORLD

### IF YOU CAN'T JUDGE A BOOK BY ITS COVER...

If you were in charge of the library, how would you arrange the books? Perhaps you're a bit lazy and might be tempted to just shelve each book that is returned in the nearest open space. Pretty soon people would be complaining that everything was mixed up and that they couldn't find the books they wanted. You need some kind of organization, or classification. If you sorted the books according to size or the color of the covers, the

shelves might look nice, but they wouldn't be very useful to people wanting to borrow books. Arranging the books alphabetically according to author would make it possible to find other books by a favorite author but not books on a particular subject. Alphabetical arrangement according to titles might help a little, but if you were looking for a book on frogs you would miss titles like *The Bug Zapper's Guide* and *Life on a Lily Pad*. So libraries use a very orderly classification system—the Dewey decimal system or the Library of Congress system. Every subject group has its own unique division. Can you think of other ways to classify the books in a library?

# PLANTS WERE THE PIONEERS

What would the earth look like if there were no life on it? On all the lands, bare rock or sand would stretch out for miles. Nowhere would there be a touch of green or any flicker of movement other than dust stirred up by the wind. Scientists believe that our planet actually was very much like that through nearly 90 percent of its long history—for billions of years, even after living things had already appeared in the seas.

At last, they say, about 400 million years ago sea creatures began to invade the lands and make their homes there. The first invaders were all plants; soon they were followed by animals that fed on plants, and they, in turn, became a source of food for other animals that came out of the sea.

Scientists have built up a picture of our planet's history by studying fossils—the remains of ancient organisms that happened to be preserved in one way or another—and comparing them to the plants, animals, and other creatures that are living now. To do this effectively, they had to have ways of sorting out the great diversity of living things, cataloging and comparing their similarities and differences.

## SORTING THINGS OUT

Scientists have observed and described nearly two million different kinds of living things. But no one knows how many kinds there really are on earth, or how many have become extinct. Each year 7,000 to 10,000 new species are identified and named—and from 17,500 to 50,000 species become extinct.

Imagine trying to learn about that many creatures! How could you keep all their names straight, much less remember the important facts about them? One way would be to find patterns and relationships. Similar types of organisms could be grouped together and compared to other groups. Biologists have been doing just that for many centuries. Each new creature that is discovered is fitted into the group that is the best match for it; it is classified.

**Classification** is the process of dividing objects into related groups. **Taxonomy** is the science of classifying or arranging living things into groups based on characteristics they share. It comes from the Greek words *taxis*, which means "arrangement," and *nomos*, which means "law."

The classification system biologists use today is based on the one devised by the eighteenth-century Swedish botanist and naturalist Carl Linnaeus. Each living thing is given a two-part name based on some of its most important characteristics. The first

*Carl Linnaeus (1707–1778) devised the scientific method of naming living things. He wrote books in Latin on the classification of plants and animals.*

name corresponds to the **genus**, a group of rather closely related kinds of organisms. The second name, the **species**, identifies the particular kind of creature within the genus. For example, *Cucurbita maxima* (winter squash), *Cucurbita pepo pepo* (pumpkin), and *Cucurbita pepo condensa* (summer squash) all make good eating, but only *Cucurbita pepo pepo* is used for making jack-o'-lanterns for Halloween and pumpkin pies for Thanksgiving. *Cucurbita pepo ovifera* (gourd) is not good to eat but was used by Native Americans to make bottles, scoops, and rattles. They all belong to the same genus. They are related organisms that have many things in common, but they have enough differences to be considered as separate species.

Each successive group in the classification, from kingdom to species, contains a smaller number of organisms that are more closely related to one another. **Division** Anthophyta, for example, contains all of the flowering plants, from grass (did you know grass has flowers?) to tulips and roses to towering trees such as oak, maple, and palm trees. Within this division, plants are grouped into two large classes: Dicotyledones (including roses, oaks, and beans) and Monocotyledones (such as grasses, lilies, and palms).

---

**MEMORY AIDS**

Silly sentences can help you remember lists. The first letters of

**K**eep **D**aisy **C**hains **O**ff **F**ine **G**rass **S**kirts

can help you remember the major groups of the scientific system for classifying plants:

**K**ingdom, **D**ivision, **C**lass, **O**rder, **F**amily, **G**enus, **S**pecies.

(Divisions in the plant kingdom correspond to groups called phyla in the other kingdoms of life.)

*White oak* (Quercus alba), *shown here in flower, is slow growing but lives a long time.*

Scientific names often describe a characteristic of an organism. Guess what color elephant grass (*Pennisetum purpureum*) is! *Dendrocalamus giganteus* is the tallest of all bamboos, growing up to 120 feet (36.5 meters) high. Sometimes a species is named after a person, or after the country it comes from—for example, *Camellia sinensis*, the tea plant (*sinensis* means "Chinese").

# 2

# THE PLANT KINGDOM

**W**hat is the largest creature that ever lived? A dinosaur? The blue whales that swim in the oceans today are larger than any dinosaur that ever walked the earth. The largest

*The General Sherman Tree is a giant sequoia. It is estimated to weigh more than thirty times the weight of the largest blue whale ever recorded.*

whale recorded was 109 feet (33 meters) long and weighed about 200 tons; but the giant sequoias and redwood trees of California grow far larger than that. A sequoia named the General Sherman Tree is more than 270 feet (82 meters) tall and measures more than 100 feet (30.5 meters) around the base of its trunk. Its weight is estimated at about 6,000 tons! Some redwoods grow to more than 350 feet (103.6 meters) tall, although their trunks are not as broad. These giants belong to the plant kingdom. The other 400,000 or so species of plants that have already been observed and named include a great diversity of creatures, from giant trees down to tiny pond-living duckweeds just 0.02 inch (0.5 millimeter) across.

# WHAT IS A PLANT?

Despite their diversity, plants share a number of features in common. They are made up of many **cells**, which are interconnected and modified into a number of different types that work together for the welfare of the organism as a whole. On the microscopic level, each plant cell is surrounded not only by a thin, flexible **cell membrane** but also by a tough, stiff **cell wall** made of a natural polymer called **cellulose**. (Cotton fiber is nearly pure cellulose.) Unlike most animals, plants cannot move from place to place; they are usually rooted in a single spot and spend their lives there. But nearly all plants have an ability that animals lack: they make their own food from simple raw materials (water and carbon dioxide, a gas from the air), using a green substance called **chlorophyll** to trap the energy from sunlight. In this process, called **photosynthesis**, the raw materials are converted first to sugars and then stored as starches. In general, plants reproduce sexually, mingling the hereditary information from two parents, but they can also reproduce in various asexual ways, producing offspring just like their single parent.

For a long time taxonomists divided the world of life into only two kingdoms: plants and animals. But there were many creatures that did not fit neatly into such a simple classification. Mushrooms and other fungi, for example, are plantlike in some ways, but they are not green and do not make their own food. Some tiny water-dwelling creatures are green and make their own food, but they swim around actively like animals; others have a plantlike life but their bodies are made up of only a single cell, or of groups of similar cells that remain together but are not interconnected.

Most modern taxonomists recognize the existence of five major kingdoms of life: Monera (bacteria and other primitive single-celled forms), Protista (single-celled

*Some animals, such as horses, have enzymes that break down cellulose so they can eat grass, but humans cannot digest cellulose.*

animal- and plantlike creatures), Fungi, Plantae, and Animalia. But not all agree on where to draw the lines between groups. Some botanists claim three groups of algae—the brown, red, and green algae—as the first members of the plant kingdom. Others say they belong in kingdom Protista with the rest of the algae, and that is where this series places them.

## WHERE THE PLANTS CAME FROM

Whether the green algae belong to the plant kingdom or to the protists, biologists generally agree that they were the direct ancestors of the true plants. About 400 million years ago, some of the green algae living in the shallow water at the edges of the seas developed the ability to survive out on the bare land. There were advantages to living there—less competition (at least at first) and direct sunlight that allowed them to make plenty of food. But living on land brought new problems. Air does not provide the support for a plant's body that water does, and a plant surrounded by air is in constant danger of drying out. The sex cells in a water plant could readily swim to meet each other, but out on the land new ways to bring male and female cells together were needed.

The first plants were mostly small and could live only very close to the water's edge. Gradually, as the land plants became more diverse, some of them developed effective supporting structures, ways of conserving moisture, and new strategies for reproduction. The classification of present-day plant species actually follows the successive stages of the plant kingdom's adaptation to life on land.

# THE PLANT "FAMILY TREE"

Modern taxonomists generally recognize ten major divisions of the plant kingdom:

Bryophyta: mosses, liverworts, and hornworts
Psilophyta: whisk ferns
Lycophyta: club mosses
Sphenophyta: horsetails
Pterophyta: ferns
Cycadophyta: cycads
Ginkgophyta: ginkgo
Gnetophyta: gnetum, ephedra, and welwitschia
Coniferophyta: conifers (pine, spruce, redwoods, etc.)
Anthophyta: flowering plants

Oddly enough, nearly all the plants with which you are most familiar—the grasses; shade trees; and producers of fruits, vegetables, and grains—belong to just one division, Anthophyta. The flowering plants are the species with the most adaptations to life on land (although a few have returned to the water). Their division is divided in turn into two large classes: dicots (fruits, vegetables, and most trees) and monocots (grasses, lilies, and orchids). In the chapters that follow, we'll learn more about the many kinds of plants.

## JUDGMENT CALLS

Animal biologists define a species as a group of closely related organisms that have many characteristics in common and can breed with other individuals in the group to produce fertile offspring. But the situation is somewhat different for plants. Members of the same species, growing in different places or bred by people for particular qualities, may look and act quite differently. (Would you think, for example, that yellow crookneck squashes and deep-green zucchinis are fruits of the same species?) And plants of different species can often crossbreed successfully to produce fertile hybrids. (Triticale, for example, is a hybrid of wheat and rye.) Where to draw the species lines is often a matter of individual judgment. If botanists followed the same rules as animal taxonomists, the total number of identified plant species might be much larger (or smaller)!

# 3

## HUMBLE BEGINNINGS

Small green plants that are only partly adapted to life on land are called **bryophytes** (division Bryophyta). Their name comes from Greek words meaning "sprouting leaf," and they have short stems and green leaves containing chlorophyll.

### WATER CHILDREN

Bryophytes live in moist areas and are fastened to the ground by rootlike structures called **rhizoids**. These rhizoids are just anchors; they do not absorb water or minerals as the roots of higher plants do. Instead, the entire plant soaks up the water and nutrients from the ground when it rains.

Bryophytes also reveal their water-plant ancestry in another way. The sperm needs to swim through water in order to fertilize the egg. So these plants reproduce sexually after a rain or a heavy dew; when the climate is dry, reproduction is delayed until it rains again. The living bryophytes include about 15,000 species of mosses and 10,000 species of liverworts.

### WHICH IS WHICH?

**Liverworts** are easily identified by their liver-shaped body. These small plants, measuring less than 0.5 inch (about 1 centimeter) tall, grow flat on the ground in damp, shady environments.

**Mosses** are usually found close together in large groups that spread out like mats. Unlike liverworts, mosses do not lie flat on the ground; their short stems lift their delicate leaves a few inches above the ground.

*Liverworts are small, flowerless plants that spread by means of spores. Gardeners often think of them as weeds.*

Bryophytes reproduce in two ways: through single cells called **spores** or sex cells called **gametes**. The spore grows into a young plant called the **gametophyte**. The gametophyte produces sperm and eggs (male and female sex cells), which unite to form a small, new plant attached to the old plant. The **sporophyte** (the new plantlet) produces spores, which are released when they mature and are carried away by the wind. The wind scatters the spores to new places, where they may form new gametophytes. This process is called **alternation of generations**.

Bryophytes are unique in the plant kingdom. Their division is the only one in which the gametophyte is the larger plant and the sporophytes are actually parasites, dependent on the gametophytes.

*This hairy cap moss has produced tall sporophytes, which are about ready to release spores.*

## MOSSES ARE IMPORTANT

Mosses are very important in the lives of small animals. Some spiders and mites depend on mosses for shelter, and some birds use the fiber from mosses to build their nests. These plants are also vital to the whole ecosystem. They store minerals and other nutrients. After mosses die, they decompose and release the nutrients, allowing other plants to use these materials to grow.

# 4

## THE VASCULAR BREAKTHROUGH

As long as 350 million years ago, **ferns** (division **Pterophyta**) covered the land, making them one of the oldest plants. About 12,000 species of ferns are still thriving today. They are large plants that have real roots, stems, and leaves and usually live in damp, shady areas. Their leaves (called **fronds**) are long and lacy and consist of hundreds of tiny leaflets. Some ferns are less elaborate and have simple, rounded leaves.

### AN ANCIENT INVENTION

How can ferns grow so much larger than mosses and liverworts? Ferns have a **vascular system**, an arrangement of tubes running from their roots up the stems to the leaves. The roots take in water, which travels up the stems and then to the leaves. The stems also store the food ferns need to grow.

Like mosses, ferns reproduce through an alternation of generations. But in ferns the sporophytes are large, independent plants (what we normally think of as ferns), and the gametophytes are small, inconspicuous plants completely separate from the sporophyte generation. Ferns have two types of leaves: fertile and sterile. The fertile leaves bear **sporangia**, special structures that produce fern spores. The sterile leaves do not bear sporangia; they just work to make food for the plant. When the sporangia release spores, they fall to the ground. The spores then germinate, growing into small gametophyte plants, which produce male

*There are 360 species of ferns that grow naturally in North America. The cinnamon fern (Osmunda cinnamomea) grows to a height of 4-6 feet (1.2-1.8 meters). It has fertile fronds in the center that produce spores.*

and female gametes (sex cells). The male gametes need water to swim to the female gametes and begin fertilization, thus forming new sporophyte plants.

Ferns do not have any great economic use today, but the ferns and other primitive vascular plants that lived about 300 million years ago are still having a major impact on our world. Those plants were mostly huge trees that grew in swampy areas. When they died they were covered by swamp water, which prevented wood-rotting bacteria and fungi from decomposing them completely. The seas periodically flooded the swamps, and layers of sediment built up over the buried vegetation. With time, heat and pressure converted the plant material to coal and other fossil fuels.

## MORE LIVING FOSSILS

**Club mosses** (division Lycophyta) have small, scalelike leaves and stems with branches that spread out like fans. Club mosses are not real mosses, though they look like them. The *club* in their name comes from the conelike shape of their reproductive leaves. They are often called ground pine because they resemble little pine trees. The 1,000 or so species living today are the survivors of droughts that killed off the giant tree lycopods about 280 million years ago. Most belong to two genera, *Lycopodium* and *Selaginella*.

**Horsetails** (division Sphenophyta) are the last survivors of another ancient group of vascular plants. The fifteen living species belong to a single genus, *Equisetum*. (*Equus* is the Latin word for "horse.") They are usually found in vacant lots and along railroad tracks. Horsetails contain large amounts of silica (sand). They have been nicknamed scouring rushes because early settlers used them to scour pots and pans.

Some botanists call *Psilotum*, one of the two surviving genera of **whisk ferns** (division Psilophyta), a living fossil because it is so similar to the earliest vascular plants. Others believe it is a fern that lost its leaves in the course of evolution. Its simple structure consists of branching green stems, which bear knoblike sporangia. These release spores that germinate into tiny gametophytes, which live underground and feed on nutrients produced by soil fungi.

# 5

## THE FIRST SEED PLANTS

Seed-producing plants that do not have flowers are called **gymnosperms**. Their name means "naked seed"; their seeds have no outer shell and are hidden between the scales of a **cone**. Most gymnosperms are evergreens and keep their leaves year-round. Together with the ferns and other primitive vascular plants, gymnosperms once dominated the ancient forests, but now fewer than a thousand species remain.

Some species of gymnosperms have both male and female reproductive structures on the same plant. In others the individual plants are either male or female, not both. Either way, reproduction takes place in the same manner. The male cones release a cloud of **pollen** and then disintegrate. The pollen grains, which contain the male gametophytes (sperm cells), are carried off by the wind. When a pollen grain lands on a female cone, it sprouts a pollen tube that grows until it reaches the female gametophyte (egg cell). It takes nearly fourteen months before the sperm cell is able to swim over to the egg cell through a water chamber provided by the female gametophyte. The sperm and egg finally unite, and fertilization begins. The fertilized egg becomes enclosed in a seed and then develops into a tiny young plant. The seed is released when the female cone matures and its scales separate. Gymnosperms include four major divisions: the conifers, cycads, ginkgo, and gnetophytes.

### THE CHRISTMAS TREE CLAN

**Conifers** (division Coniferophyta) are cone-bearing plants that carry their seeds in cones rather than in pods or fruit. This is the largest surviving division of the gymnosperms, with 50 genera and more than 700 living species. They include trees and shrubs such as redwoods, pines, firs, spruce, hemlocks, and cypresses. Conifers can withstand extremely cold conditions because their sap produces a kind of "antifreeze" substance that allows it to continue transporting nutrients even in subfreezing temperatures. This gives conifers their strong piney smell.

Most conifer plants produce both male and female cones. The male cones are located in clusters on some lower branches, whereas the female cones can be found on higher branches. Conifer wood is used to make furniture, paper, and even plastics. Tar, oils, and turpentine are made from the **resin**, or sticky substance secreted from the tree.

*A cluster of male cones on the Ponderosa pine* (Pinus ponderosa)

Pine trees are popular evergreens with needlelike leaves, interesting pine cones, and a refreshing piney smell. They differ from other conifers by the way their leaves grow. Pine needles usually grow in bundles of two, three, or five. Other conifers grow their needles in larger bundles or do not have any bundles at all. Pine trees are considered to be the world's most important source of timber, producing fine-quality wood.

The pine family (Pinaceae) also includes spruce and fir trees. These trees look a lot alike. In fact, the spruce is more closely related to the fir than any other conifer. They are also both popular choices as Christmas trees. There are some key differences, however. Spruce needles are usually four-sided with little woody pegs that join the needles at the twig. Fir needles do not have these peglike projections. Another difference is easy to spot: the cones of spruces hang downward, whereas the cones of firs point upward. The scales on spruce cones stay on the cones; those of firs fall off when the cones ripen.

Redwood trees are among the tallest trees in the world. They grow between 200 and 275 feet (61 and 83.8 meters) high with trunks that are 8 to 12 feet (2.4 to 3.65 meters) wide. They thrive in foggy climates on the West Coast, from central California to southern Oregon and rarely grow inland. They are sometimes called coast or California redwoods so that they are not mistaken for their relatives, the giant sequoias.

The redwood is remarkable not only for its amazing height but also for its reddish-brown bark, which resists insects, fungus, and fire. Redwoods are used in construction and furniture making. Older trees produce burls (lumps) on their trunks, which are sometimes used to make bowls and other items because of their attractive grain.

Junipers, cedars, and other members of the cyprus family (Cupressaceae) have small needles that grow in pairs. Juniper seeds have a fleshy covering that makes them look like berries, but they are not true fruits. The reddish wood of the eastern red cedar (*Juniperus virginiana*) is used for storage chests and aromatic chips that protect woolen clothes from moths. Other cyprus woods are burned as incense.

## FROM DINOSAUR TIMES

*A cycad* (Encephalartos gratus) *mature seed cone*

About one hundred species of **cycads** (division Cycadophyta) survive from the age of dinosaurs. They are found naturally only in the tropics and subtropical regions. Cycads look similar to palms or ferns, but they are gymnosperms and reproduce by cones rather than flowers. The **strobilus**, a large cone that contains seeds, stands upright in the center of a circle of leaves. When the seeds mature, the strobilus withers away, and the seeds fall to the ground, where they germinate (sprout) into new plants. Cycads are either male or female, but never both.

## ONLY ONE LEFT

The **ginkgo** (division Ginkgophyta) is a real living fossil. The whole division consists of just one species, *Ginkgo biloba*, which no longer grows wild anywhere in the world. Just like its ancestors that lived about 180 million years ago, the ginkgo tree has fan-shaped leaves and grows from 60 to 80 feet (18 to 24.3 meters) tall. (It is sometimes called the maidenhair tree because its leaves look like those of a maidenhair fern.) Ginkgoes have been cultivated in China and Japan since the tenth century. Today they are popular trees on city streets in the United States because they are more resistant than other shade trees to damage by air pollution. Interestingly, only male ginkgo trees are planted in cities. The reason is that female trees produce seeds with a fleshy covering that is irritating to some people's skin and quickly rots, smelling like rancid butter. Ginkgoes are gymnosperms, but they are not evergreen. Their leaves turn golden yellow in the autumn and then drop off, leaving the branches bare through the winter.

The ginkgo tree usually grows to 35-60 feet (11-18 meters) tall and is virtually immune to diseases and pests.

## LEFTOVERS

Division Gnetophyta is a sort of catchall division that includes about seventy species in three genera that have little in common except that all are gymnosperms. The forty species of *Ephedra* are shrubs with jointed stems and scalelike leaves. Extracts from two of the species are used as drugs for asthma, emphysema, and hay fever. *Gnetum* is a genus with thirty species of vines, woody shrubs, and trees that grow in Asia, Africa, and Central and South America. The oldest and oddest member of this group is welwitschia. Its only living species, *Welwitschia mirabilis*, is found in southwestern African deserts. It is a low-growing cone-bearing plant that produces only two leaves in its one-hundred-year lifetime. Each leaf shreds as it grows, giving the appearance of multiple leaves. This plant has a wide, short stem that can store a large amount of water to help it survive through long periods of drought.

*Welwitschia growing in a dry riverbed in the Namib desert in Namibia, Africa*

# 6

# THE FLOWERING PLANTS

Flowering plants, in which the seeds are covered by a fruit, are **angiosperms** (division **Anthophyta**). The 350,000 or so species of angiosperms are classified according to differences in their leaves, flowers, and fruits.

Unlike the narrow needles of conifers, the leaves of flowering plants may be quite broad. This provides a much greater surface for gathering sunlight energy, but also a greater area for losing water by evaporation. Angiosperms have several ways of reducing water loss. Their leaves are coated with a waxy cuticle that holds in moisture. But there have to be openings to admit gases from the air—the carbon dioxide needed for photosynthesis and the oxygen needed for respiration. These openings, called **stomates**, are found on the underside of the leaf, and they can be closed off by special "guard cells" when the plant is in danger of dehydration.

## A WORLD OF DIFFERENCES

Angiosperm leaves may be simple (made up of a single leaf blade) or compound (composed of a number of small leaflets); their shape and arrangement are commonly used to tell one plant species from another. Also, a distinguishing characteristic is the pattern of the **veins**, the bundles of conducting tubes that carry water and other materials through the leaves. Most angiosperms lose their leaves every fall. The dying leaves start turning shades of red, orange, gold, and brown as the green chlorophyll begins to disintegrate and red and yellow pigments also present in the leaves can be seen.

The other main parts of the plant—stems and roots—also differ from one species to another. Stems may be slender green tubes, supported only by the plumping effect of the fluids held inside their cellulose cell walls. Other angiosperms have woody trunks,

*Lily of the Valley* (right) *has a single broad leaf, while the Marigold* (far right) *has a compound leaf made up of a number of small leaflets.*

reinforced by a firm structure of lignins and other wood chemicals. Some plants that live in dry regions have thick fleshy stems specially adapted to store reserves of water.

Roots are another distinguishing feature. Plants such as carrots, beets, and dandelions have a single broad root, called a **taproot**; other plants, such as corn and beans, have multiple branching roots that spread out over a wide area.

Leaves, stems, and roots form the sporophyte in angiosperms. The gametophyte, as in the gymnosperms, consists of the male and female cells (pollen and ovule), produced in specialized reproductive organs—**flowers**. Seeds develop inside the closed ovary, which forms a **fruit**. This is the source of the name *angiosperm*, which means "covered seed."

Many angiosperms have brightly colored or sweet-smelling flowers, which

## HOW FLOWERS MAKE FRUITS

The male parts of the flower, which are located closest to the petals, are the **stamens**. This is where the pollen grains are produced. They contain the sperm cells. Each stamen has a thin stalk called a **filament**. At the top of the filament is an **anther**. The anther produces the pollen.

In the center of the flower are the female parts, called the **pistils**. The lower part of the pistil contains the **ovary**, which produces **ovules** that hold the eggs. The top of the pistil, called the **stigma**, is covered with a sticky substance.

When pollen grains land on the stigma, they sprout. A hollow tube grows down the pistil from each pollen grain until it reaches the ovary. Sperm travel down the pollen tubes and join with the eggs. This process is called **fertilization**. Then the ovary ripens into a fruit with seeds inside it.

*A white-lined sphinx moth gathers nectar. Insects play an important role in plant fertilization by spreading pollen from flower to flower.*

attract insects, particularly bees. The insects feed on the pollen and nectar (sugary liquid secreted by special cells in some flowers) and, in traveling from one flower to another, transfer pollen and help to fertilize the ovules. Animals also feed on plant fruits. This is actually beneficial for the plants, helping to spread their seeds to new areas.

## WHAT'S THE DIFFERENCE?

If you soak a dried bean seed overnight and then carefully take it apart, you will find a tiny plantlet, with leaves and a root, hidden inside the two large fleshy halves of the bean. The fleshy parts are the **cotyledons**, which contain stored food to support the plant while it is germinating and beginning to grow. Beans, as well as the majority of other angiosperm species, have two cotyledons—they are **dicots**. (The prefix *di-* means "two.") If you carefully remove a corn kernel from a corncob and peel off its seed coat, you will not find two cotyledons. Corn, like other **monocots**, has just a single cotyledon in its seeds. (*Mono-* means "one.")

The fossil records show that the dicots developed first and were later followed by the monocots. In addition to the difference in their seeds, the two classes of flowering plants have a number of other distinguishing features:

| DICOTS | MONOCOTS |
|---|---|
| Flower parts in multiples of two, four, or five | Flower parts in multiples of three |
| Long, tapering leaves with a network of veins | Broad or narrow leaves with parallel veins |
| Vascular bundles in stems are arranged in a circle | Vascular bundles in stems are scattered |

*Runner bean plants are dicots. Bean plants have leaves with a network of veins.*

*Corn plants are monocots. These plants typically have leaves with parallel veins.*

## TIME IS RUNNING OUT

When the topic of endangered species comes up, animals like tigers or spotted owls usually grab the headlines. Actually, though, many plant species are endangered, too. Botanists believe that about 3,000 species of plants in the United States are in danger, and about 40,000 plant species around the world may soon be extinct.

When people ask why we should care about losing some of the many living species on earth, the answers are usually rather sentimental. But the loss of plant species may be a disaster for very practical reasons. More than a quarter of the medications prescribed today (including 77 percent of the 150 most prescribed drugs) come from natural sources—mainly plants. Yet only 5 percent of all the species of flowering plants have been studied enough to determine whether they have medical value. We may lose some potential wonder drugs to extinction without even realizing it!

In the mid-1990s the Center for Plant Conservation at Harvard University began a program to collect samples of threatened species and form a "living library" of plants and seeds. The collections will provide materials for study and also for reintroducing endangered plants into natural habitats.

# 7

# BLOOMING
# BEAUTIES

All of the angiosperms make flowers, but some are much showier than others. People prize these flowering plants for their beauty and have carefully bred many species to produce larger, sweeter-smelling, and more colorful blooms. Yet many of the plants most prized for their flowers belong to families and orders that also include members known for other qualities, such as their tasty and nutritious fruits.

## THE FIRST FLOWERS

Some botanists call the division of flowering plants Magnoliophyta, and Magnoliopsida is sometimes used as a synonym for the class Dicotyledones. The members of the magnolia family are the most like the first flowering plants, preserved as fossils. The order Magnoliales includes not only magnolias but also nutmeg, pepper, and the water lily.

*Magnolia trees produce large, showy blossoms.*

**Magnolias** (family Magnoliaceae) are beautiful trees with remarkably large leaves and milky-white flowers that give off a sweet smell that fills the air with a hint of lemon. The Southern magnolia, which is an evergreen, has become a symbol of hospitality in the Deep South of the United States. The magnolia is both the state tree and the state flower of Mississippi as well as the state flower of Louisiana. Other types of magnolias are planted where the weather is not as warm and are deciduous (that is, they lose their leaves in the autumn). The saucer magnolia, for example, produces colored flowers and comes from China.

Those "lily pads" that frogs love to sit on are really the broad leaves of water lilies (family Nymphaeaceae). They are also called pond lilies because they are usually found floating in ponds. Water lilies have waxy rounded leaves that spread out on the water surface. Their long stalks are attached to enormous rootlike stems, which are buried in the mud at the bottom of the pond. The stalks produce pretty flowers of different colors, although the white-flowered water lily is the most popular. These decorative flowers provide food for fish and other water animals, but they grow so rapidly that they can cause drainage problems.

*This underwater view of water lilies shows the long stalks that attach them to a root system at the bottom of a pond.*

## THE BUTTERCUP CLAN

Did you ever put a buttercup (family Ranunculaceae) up to your face to see if it made a yellow reflection, indicating that you like butter? Large numbers of buttercups pop up every year in the springtime. This bright yellow flower was named for its color and its cuplike shape. The buttercup is also known as the crowfoot because its petals are like the birds' feet. You may think of buttercups as attractive "fun" flowers, but farmers and cattle wouldn't agree. Cattle and horses rarely eat buttercups because they contain a very unpleasant, bitter juice and can even be poisonous if enough of them are eaten. Farmers consider these flowers an overgrown nuisance, especially since they compete with more useful plants for growing space.

Larkspurs (Delphinium) are named for the distinctive shape of their flowers. Wild larkspurs are also known as locoweed because sheep and cattle that eat these plants begin to stagger and may even die. Horticulturists usually use the name *larkspurs* only for annual delphiniums (those that flower and die and must be replanted from seeds the next year). They use the name *delphiniums* for the perennial kinds, which regrow new leaves and flowers from the same roots.

The buttercups' subclass Ranunculidae also includes an important family whose main claim to fame is not based on their beautiful flowers. These are the poppies

*The Oriental poppy* (Papaver orientale) *blooms for a short time in early summer. It produces large, colorful flowers.*

(family Papaveraceae). If you have colorful poppies growing in your garden, they are probably California or common poppies. In the United States it is illegal to grow the kind of poppies that produce a milky white juice containing a powerful drug, **opium**. This poppy's scientific name, *Papaver somniferum*, literally means "sleep-bringing poppy." Opium and chemicals produced from it, such as morphine and heroin, can put people to sleep or relieve pain. It has been widely used for medical purposes but has also been abused as a mood-altering drug. Smoking or injecting opium can lead to serious addictions to this drug.

Most poppies don't have any narcotic properties. These flowers have a number of uses. The tiny poppy seeds are often sold to feed birds. Oil extracted from the flower is sometimes used in preparing foods. And, of course, poppy seeds are used to add flavor to breads, rolls, and other foods.

## BLOOMING HEADS

The composite family (Compositae) includes a large variety of dicot flowering plants. Each flower head is a **composite** (combination) of small flowers. The heads are usually made up of two kinds of flowers—ray and disk flowers. The ray flowers come out of the disk or tubular flowers, like the rays coming out of the sun. Common composite plants include daisy, thistle, dandelion, and sunflower. A few composite plants, such as lettuce and artichokes, are used as food by humans.

The daisy's flower is yellow and shaped like a disk. Around the edge, a group of ray flowers surround the disk. The "rays" may be white, pink, red, or purple. The leaves are bunched together at the bottom of the stem, leaving the stalk bare. The name *daisy* comes from Old English words meaning "day's eye." This referred to the fact that the daisy blossoms close at night and open up at dawn, just like an eye.

*A daisy is a composite flowering plant. It has a disk flower in the center surrounded by ray flowers.*

Thistles are annoying weeds that have sharp, prickly leaves but soft, delicate flowers. The heads of the flowers, which are thick and contain no ray flowers, form large balls of seeds that are dispersed by the wind. Thistles can reproduce quickly for this reason. These plants growing in pastures and fields are a nuisance to farmers.

The dandelion is another weed that multiplies quickly. It got its name from the French phrase *dent de lion*, which means "lion's tooth." The dandelion has smooth leaves with rough edges, resembling teeth. The yellow dandelion head is actually a cluster of flowers. Dandelions reproduce in a unique manner—unlike other plants, the ovaries of dandelions produce fertile seeds without **pollination**. Though gardeners often consider dandelions a nuisance, their leaves are eaten in salads and their flowers can be made into dandelion wine.

Sunflower plants have huge stems, reaching up to 15 feet (4.5 meters) tall. Yellow flowers surround their large, disk-shaped heads. In the wild, the heads may grow up to 6 inches (15 centimeters) wide. When they're cultivated, they can reach 1 foot (30 centimeters) or more and produce up to 1,000 seeds. Sunflowers can turn their heads and face the sun throughout the day.

*Sunflowers belong to the genus* Helianthus.

Sunflowers are valued for their seeds, which are high in protein and can be enjoyed dried or roasted. People also stock up on sunflower seeds to feed the birds throughout the winter. A sweet vegetable oil can be extracted from sunflower seeds and is used in making margarine and cooking oil. Sunflower oil is also sometimes used in soap and paint.

# 8

# GOOD TO EAT

Nutrition experts agree that most Americans don't eat enough fruits and vegetables. These plant products contain valuable nutrients—not only the body's basic fuels and building materials (carbohydrates, fats, and proteins) but also vitamins, minerals, and other chemicals that researchers believe may help to keep people healthy.

Most of the edible dicots belong to two large subclasses: Dilleniidae, which includes cabbage and its relatives and the cucurbits (cucumbers and squashes), as well as a number of trees (such as the willow) and flowers including peonies and violets; and Rosidae, which was named for the roses but also includes apples, beans, citrus fruits, grapes, and olives, along with trees such as maple and dogwood.

## MARVELOUS MUSTARDS

We often think of mustard as that spicy hot condiment we put on our hotdogs. This table mustard is actually created by curing the seeds produced by the mustard plant. But spreading some hot, spicy mustard on a ham sandwich isn't the only thing mustard is good for. The mustard plant is also enjoyed as a vegetable. Its large, dark-green leaves

### NATURE'S CANCER FIGHTERS

When former President George Bush announced that he didn't like broccoli, he made nation-wide headlines. Nutritionists quickly advised the public that broccoli and other crucifers really are good for you. In fact, research has shown that they contain chemicals that strengthen the body's defenses against cancer.

are highly nutritious. Mustard is a great source of vitamins A, B, and C, and it contains enough bulk and fiber to have a slight laxative effect.

Members of the mustard family (**Cruciferae**) have four petals that form the shape of a cross, as its name (which means "cross-bearing") indicates. This family includes a large variety of garden vegetables such as cabbage, broccoli, cauliflower, and turnips. (These varied vegetables—and mustard, too—are quite closely related; all are species in the genus *Brassica*.) Like mustard, these vegetables are also nutritionally beneficial. However, cabbage, broccoli, and cauliflower are known for being very gas-producing foods and may be difficult to digest.

*Black mustard* (Brassica nigra) *in flower*

Broccoli is closely related to cauliflower. Both have thick clusters of flower buds that form edible "heads." However, the heads of broccoli are green and more branched-out and open than those of cauliflower. The heads of cauliflower are white, round, and clumped together.

Cabbage has pale green leaves that overlap one another, forming a single hard, round head. Cabbage is used in various foods. Shredded cabbage is the main ingredi-

*A selection of members of the* Brassica *genus: broccoli, cabbage, kale, Brussels sprouts, turnips, and others*

ent of coleslaw. Cabbage soup is popular in many parts of Europe. Red cabbage is very attractive, and its leaves are filled with purplish veins. It is sometimes used in salads to add some color.

Turnips have edible greens, too, but they are grown mainly for their roots, which are round and firm and weigh up to 1 pound (450 grams) each. Turnip roots may be eaten boiled or mashed and are a good source of vitamin C. (The leaves, like those of other crucifers, are rich in iron and vitamin A.)

Recently researchers have discovered that some plants, especially the Indian mustard (*Brassica juncea*), are able to take up large amounts of metal from the soil or water. They believe the plants use this metal-accumulating ability as a defense against insects and disease germs. Now researchers hope to use superaccumulating plants to clean up the soil at toxic waste dumps.

## SOME ROSES TASTE GOOD

We all know the rose is a beautiful flower. People often receive roses on special holidays, such as Valentine's Day or anniversaries. Roses are notable for their sweet smell and their striking appearance. They grow on bushes or on climbing vines, with sharp thorns to protect them. Roses come in a large variety of colors, to which people often give special meanings. For instance, a red rose is a symbol of love; a white one is a symbol of friendship; and a yellow one is traditionally from a secret admirer.

Members of the rose family (**Rosaceae**) are good for more than just looking and smelling nice. This family also includes trees that produce some of our favorite fruits: apples, cherries, plums, peaches, pears, and almonds. Strawberry vines also belong to the rose family.

The apple tree produces beautiful white flowers that look like tiny roses when they blossom. The fruits come in various colors—red, yellow, and green. Their core contains many seeds. Apples have become a favorite of all the fruits, eaten raw for snacks or made into various

*This "Electron" rose is a hybrid tea rose. The wild roses are the true species. Fossil remains in Europe and America show that the rose existed long before humans.*

desserts, jellies, and baked goods. The old saying, "An apple a day keeps the doctor away," isn't far from the truth. Apples contain important vitamins we need every day, like vitamins A and C, and also minerals such as potassium.

Pears come in many shapes, but they usually have a round bottom and taper at the top to the stem. Pears are more closely related to apples than any other fruit. They have cores similar to those of apples, containing up to ten seeds each. Some types of pears taste rather sandy because they contain little grit cells. Other pears, such as the European pears, don't taste so gritty because they only have a few grit cells.

Plums are sometimes sweet and sometimes sour, depending on how ripe they are. The riper, or softer they are, the sweeter they taste. This juicy fruit has a single hard pit in the center, which contains one or two seeds. Some varieties of plum are dried to make prunes. Actually, the genus name of plums is *Prunus* (the garden plum is *Prunus domestica*), but the same genus also includes a number of other "stone fruits"—for example, the sweet cherry (*P. avium*), the sour cherries used in pies (*P. cerasus*), the apricot (*P. armeniaca*), the peach (*P. persica*), and the almond (*P. amygdalus*). Each has a single hard pit containing one or two seeds.

Ordinary cherries are usually red, but the sweet Bing cherry is almost black. Some types are sour, but the majority of cherry trees planted produce sweet cherries.

Peach trees grow most successfully in very hot weather. Peaches are usually picked by hand to avoid bruising. They have a soft furlike skin often known as peach fuzz. When peaches are ripe, they become very juicy.

The almond tree has long, pointy leaves with pretty pink flowers. The flesh of its fruits is too leathery to eat; the tree is grown for its tasty seeds. Some almond trees bear

*A plum (far right), genus* Prunus, *has a hard pit with one or two seeds. An apple (right), genus* Malus, *has a core containing several seeds.*

bitter almonds and others have sweet almonds. The sweet almonds are the ones we eat salted, roasted, or added to baked items such as cookies and pastries. The bitter almonds are not edible. They contain amygdalin, a poisonous substance that releases hydrogen cyanide when it is digested. (Peach seeds are also bitter and poisonous.)

Strawberries are not real berries, like blueberries or cranberries. True berries have their seeds inside the fruit, but strawberries are covered with seeds on the outside of their heart-shaped bodies. In a strawberry patch, leaves grow from the strawberry stems. The strawberries look like they were strewn (scattered) within the batch of leaves and were once called strewberry. At some point the spelling changed to *strawberry*.

## NATURE'S FERTILIZER

**Legumes** belong to one of the largest families of flowering plants, Leguminosae, the pea family. Legumes include some of our most valuable food plants, as well as feed for farm animals. The legumes, which produce pods containing seeds, include peas, beans, peanuts, and clover.

Legumes have a unique partnership with nitrogen-fixing bacteria. Nodules form on the legume roots and provide shelter for the bacteria, which convert nitrogen gas from the air to nitrate salts that plants can use. (Nitrogen is an essential element in proteins, for which legumes are an excellent source.) Legume crops are thus a sort of natural fertilizer that helps to enrich the soil.

Peas and beans are very nutritious legumes. Their pods are divided lengthwise and contain a number of edible seeds. The protein they contain is much more complete than that of most other plant products. Soybeans are added to many processed foods, such as pasta, to enrich their proteins. The Japanese food tofu is a soybean product, and soy protein is also processed into artificially flavored meat substitutes.

The peanut plant is a legume that grows pods containing one or more seeds. We call the seeds peanuts, but they're not real nuts—they're more closely related to peas. The

*The pods of the peanut plant ripen underground, unlike other legumes. Peanut plants grow well in sandy loam and are an important crop in the southern United States.*

## SENSITIVE LEGUMES

The mimosa tree, or silk tree, is a decorative tree that bears a crown of delicate pink and white flowers that develop into typical legume pods. The scientific name of this tree is *Albizia julibrissin*, but there is another "mimosa"—also a legume—called *Mimosa pudica*, or the sensitive plant. If you gently touch one of its leaves, the leaflets quickly fold up. A firmer touch, and all the leaves droop, as though they were wilting. After about ten minutes the leaves lift up and spread out again. The plant also closes its leaves at night and in cold weather. But if it is exposed to ether or chloroform, it no longer responds to touch!

Ordinary bean plants also fold up their leaves at night. You can make a movie of this "plant ballet" by growing a bean seedling on a sunny windowsill and taking a picture of it every hour. (Be sure your camera is set up in exactly the same position each time.) If you put the photos in order and staple them together at the top, then flip through them quickly, you will see the bean plant raise its leaves and turn them toward the sun, then fold them up when it gets dark.

*The* Mimosa pudica *is called a sensitive plant because it closes its leaves when they are touched. This reaction is call a thigmonastic response. The plant shown above was found in Brazil.*

peanut plant is very unusual because the flowers bloom aboveground, but the pod develops underground.

Clover is a valuable source of food for farm animals. It is given to the animals in the form of hay and silage and contains large amounts of protein and minerals. There are various kinds of clovers, such as red, white, strawberry, and crimson species. Red clover is more widely used to nourish farm animals than other clovers. Alfalfa is another legume crop used as animal fodder.

# 9

## POISONS, PRICKLES, AND TRAPS

What foods do you like best? Most people's favorites are foods that taste sweet or creamy, or perhaps spicy. It's unlikely that any really bitter foods are among your favorites; in fact, children naturally dislike bitter tastes. There is an important reason for this inborn taste preference: many poisons produced by plants have bitter tastes. So people who did not eat bitter-tasting plants were more likely to survive and pass their taste traits on to their descendants.

A bad taste is only one of the defenses plants have developed against animals that might eat them. The sharp thorns that stick out from rose stems and the splinterlike spines that stud the surface of a cactus are also defensive weapons. And some plants have even gone on the offense, forming traps to catch insects and other small animals, on which the plants feed.

### A DEADLY REPUTATION

The **nightshade** family (Solanaceae) includes many toxic plants, often giving the impression that all nightshades are poisonous. That's not true. The nightshades include plants that produce some of our most popular foods, such as potatoes, tomatoes, eggplants, and peppers. Some of the poisonous nightshades include tobacco and deadly nightshade, or belladonna.

When tomatoes were first introduced into Europe, they were thought to be poisonous because they were related to poisonous nightshades. Eventually Europeans learned what the Incas of South America had long known: tomatoes are not only safe, but they're also very tasty and nutritious. They were once called love apples because of a superstition that eating tomatoes made people fall in love.

Like the tomato, the eggplant is a fruit that is mistakenly considered a vegetable. The eggplant is the largest fruit in the nightshade family and can grow up to 12 inches (about 30 centimeters) long. This purplish fruit got its name because its shape resembles that of an egg.

The peppers that belong to the nightshade family are not related to the black pepper used as a spice. (That pepper is a member of the magnolia family.) The only similarity is in the effects they produce. Some varieties of peppers, such as the chili pepper or the cayenne pepper, contain a large amount of an oleoresin called capsaicin. This chemical produces a hot, burning sensation when these

*These tomatoes are ripe and ready to be picked. Indians of Mexico grew* tomatl *long before Europeans arrived in their country. Those Indians would have trouble recognizing the hundreds of varieties of today's tomato plant.*

peppers are eaten. The most popular kind of pepper is the green bell pepper, named for its broad, bell-like shape. It is sweet and mild and contains the least amount of oleoresin. Bell peppers are often eaten raw in salads or cooked and mixed with various dishes to add flavor. When bell peppers ripen, they turn bright red but are still sweet-tasting. The hot-tasting peppers have an elongated shape, with a pointed end.

The edible parts of the potato plant are not fruits but **tubers**, enlarged portions of stems modified for storing starch and other nutrients. Potatoes are also referred to as white potatoes to distinguish them from sweet potatoes (which are roots of plants in the morning glory family). Although potatoes themselves are edible, all of the green parts of the potato plant, even green potatoes, are poisonous. The potato is a very nutritious vegetable. It's also not fattening, as long as you don't add sour cream or butter.

### TOMATO: FRUIT OR VEGETABLE?

People usually consider the tomato a vegetable, and that is how it is defined by laws, but botanists classify it as a fruit because it is actually a ripened ovary. Since tomatoes are usually eaten in salads or with the main course—as lettuce, carrots, or other vegetables are—the confusion is understandable.

It's hard to believe that potatoes are related to tomatoes (other than the fact that their names sound similar). The tomato is a juicy fruit, whereas the potato is a firm vegetable. However, the flowers on potato plants produce seed balls that look just like little green tomatoes.

After European explorers were shown by Native Americans how to smoke cured tobacco leaves in a pipe, tobacco quickly gained worldwide popularity. Yet the tobacco plant (*Nicotiana tabacum*) is one of the toxic members of the nightshade family. It produces a powerful poison, the alkaloid nicotine. One drop of this chemical in its purified state is fatal if it comes into contact with human skin. Cigarettes, cigars, pipe tobacco, snuff, and chewing tobacco are actually devices for delivering small doses of the drug. In the amounts absorbed by smoking a cigarette, nicotine can make a person feel more relaxed or more alert. Unfortunately, it is addictive. Over a period of years, smoking greatly increases the risk of heart and lung diseases. In addition to nicotine, smoking also delivers carbon monoxide, tars, and other harmful combustion products. In fact, just being near someone who is smoking can increase the health risks.

The deadly nightshade, also called belladonna, produces poisonous berries. Just three of these glossy black berries could kill a child.

*The belladonna plant is related to the potato enjoyed by so many, but belladonna produces very poisonous berries.*

## BEWARE THE ITCH

"Leaves in three, let them be" is a good saying to follow if you want to stay away from poisonous plants like poison ivy or poison oak. These three-leaf plants of the sumac family (Anacardiaceae) grow as climbing vines or shrubs and contain an allergy-causing substance that irritates the skin when touched, causing an itchy rash. An equally irritating relative, poison sumac, has leaves up to 1 foot (about 30 centimeters) long, containing seven to thirteen leaflets. People usually get this terrible rash only during the warmer months, but poison ivy is actually around all year. It's just that when the weather is cold, people are less likely to explore the woods or other areas where poison ivy is commonly located.

You may develop a rash by touching a poison ivy plant directly or even indirectly. Poison-ivy rash is sometimes called the cow itch because people can get it after touching cows or other animals that have brushed against these plants. The best thing to do is to wash your clothes and hands immediately after coming into contact with poison ivy. This will wash away any "poisonous" residue.

Another member of the same family, the cashew tree, produces nuts that also contain an irritating poison on their shells. People who touch cashew nut shells may develop skin blisters. Roasting the cashew nuts removes all the poison, and we can then enjoy this delicious kidney-shaped nut.

Pistachio nuts also belong to the sumac family, but they do not contain any irritating poison.

*Poison ivy* (Rhus radicans) *has a well-deserved bad reputation. Its leaves contain a substance that can cause an irritating rash.*

### DID YOU KNOW?

Poison ivy and poison sumac produce white berries, whereas ordinary ivy and sumac plants produce red berries.

## WELL GUARDED

Touching a **cactus** can be a very painful experience. That's because this plant is usually covered with pointy spines all around its body. Cacti, which all belong to the family

*This elf owl (*Micrathene whitneyi) *is nesting in a saguaro cactus, whose spines provide protection from predators. The saguaro may grow up to 60 feet (18 meters) tall.*

Cactaceae, thrive best in hot and dry areas, especially in Mexico and the southwestern United States. They have thick, plump stems with waxy skin. The stems absorb and store water, and the skin keeps it from evaporating. Cacti have very long roots that grow close to the surface, spreading out as much as 50 feet (15 meters) in all directions, to gather as much water as possible after it rains.

The spines of cacti come in different shapes and sizes, and some may be sharper than others. They grow out of small mounds called **areoles** on the stem. Like the spines, flowers also grow out of areoles. Some cacti bear very attractive flowers with bright colors. These flowers produce cactus berries containing seeds that are dispersed by the wind. One cactus plant can produce a million seeds during its lifetime, but only one or two seeds will live long enough to produce a new cactus plant.

Small animals, insects, and birds eat the stems and flowers of cacti. Birds build their nests in the stems. The cactus plant may also act as a refuge for birds and animals to hide from predators. People can also eat cactus stems once the spines have been scraped off, and some do eat cactus fruits. A number of cacti can be used for lumber.

## WHERE'S THE MEAT?

Besides making their own food by photosynthesis, **carnivorous** plants actually eat small animals, including insects and even tree frogs! The meat-eating plants use specialized traps to catch their prey. There are three types of carnivorous plants: the pitcher plant, sundews such as the Venus's-flytrap plant (*Dionaea muscipula*), and butterworts.

The pitcher plant has slippery, pitcher-shaped leaves that hold water. When an insect attracted by the bright colors of the leaves alights, it loses its footing and falls into the trap. The insect drowns and the pitcher plant digests it. Certain animals have outsmarted the traps, though. Pitcher-plant mosquitoes fly in and out like tiny helicopters and lay eggs in the water. The larvae feed on the remains of dead insects, then cut a hole through the leaf and escape. Some spiders spin webs across the opening, and small frogs perch just inside to catch insects attracted to the pitcher plant.

*An insect has become trapped in a pitcher plant, which will digest it over a period of time.*

The Venus's-flytrap plant actually catches its prey. This plant has special trigger hairs on each leaf that stiffen up when they are touched by an insect crawling on the leaf. When two hairs are touched (or one is touched twice), the two leaf halves snap shut over the insect, almost like teeth chomping down on the plant's victim. The leaf stays tightly closed until its prey is digested. (If it was a false alarm or the insect got away, the leaf opens up, ready to try again.)

The third kind of carnivorous plant is the butterwort. This plant has a sticky substance on the leaf surface. When an insect gets stuck, the leaf curls over the prey and then digests it. Although butterworts eat insects, they also depend on insects to pollinate their slender purple flowers. Bladderworts, which belong to a different genus in the same family (Lentibulariaceae), grow in ponds. Their leaves form underwater trapdoor chambers that catch insects and other small water animals.

# 10

## OUR LEGAL DRUGS

Some plant products that are enjoyed worldwide contain a legal drug called **caffeine**. It is a stimulant found in small amounts in coffee, tea, chocolate, and certain cola drinks.

Coffee has become a favorite hot drink in almost every country in the world. Almost all coffee comes from the coffee plant (*Coffea arabica*), which originated in Arabia but is now grown all over the world. These plants, which prefer a shady environment, are woody shrubs or small trees with waxy evergreen leaves. The coffee plant produces self-pollinating white flowers that cluster on short stalks between the leaves. The flowers develop into a bunch of berries and turn red when they are ripe. Each berry contains two seeds, or beans. The seeds are then fermented and dried and turned into the commercial product, coffee beans. When these beans are ground and brewed, they make a hot cup of coffee, famous for waking people up in the morning.

According to an old Chinese legend, the world's first cup of tea was discovered by Chinese emperor Shen-Nung in 2737 B.C. Leaves from a wild tea bush fell into a pot of his drinking water as it was being boiled. The emperor liked the taste of this interesting mixture—the first cup of tea.

The tea plant (*Camellia sinensis*) is an evergreen shrub that flourishes in warm climates. It is a member of the tea family, Theaceae. It produces tiny white flowers that contain three seeds in each flower. The leaves and flowers are collected and brewed to make tea. Tea is the second most popular beverage worldwide, after coffee. For centuries, China maintained all the tea plants. Then Japan took an interest in

*A coffee plant* (Coffea arabica) *with flowers and beans*

tea plants, and tea also became a part of Japanese daily life. Tea is gaining new popularity today, since researchers have reported that green tea and black tea may protect people against cancer.

What's the difference between green tea and black tea? All teas are made by first fermenting and then steaming the cut-off tips of branches, which usually contain a bud and two leaves. Green teas have a shorter fermentation, so some of the plant's chlorophyll still remains. Black teas are fermented longer.

Wouldn't it be great if chocolate grew on trees? Actually, it does. What is sometimes referred to as the chocolate tree is really a tropical tree called the cacao tree. This tree (*Theobroma cacao*) produces cacao beans, which are used in making chocolate. But this tree doesn't grow the sweet-tasting treat we know and love.

Chocolate was discovered by the Aztecs. They ground up the cacao beans to make a rather bitter, although popular drink called *chocolatl*. When the Spanish explorer Hernando Cortés took cacao beans back to Spain, Spanish cooks sweetened the taste by adding sugar. The sweetened chocolate became a very popular drink among the aristocrats, but it was very expensive. It was not until easier ways to grind cacao beans were invented that chocolate became cheap enough to be enjoyed by everybody.

Today most chocolate comes from cacao trees grown on small farms in tropical regions of Africa and the Americas. The trees have small flowers that produce colorful fruits or pods that look like long cucumbers. The seeds found in the pods are fermented and dried, forming cacao beans. The beans go through a special process of blending, roasting, and grinding before they become what we know as chocolate.

*A cacao tree (Theobroma cacao) with seed pods growing on a cacao farm in Brazil*

# 11

_____

# IN THE SHADE

_____

Some dicot trees are covered with beautiful blossoms each spring, and some bear nutritious fruits or nuts. But these are not the only things that make trees useful. Their spreading roots help to hold the soil together, keeping it from washing away in the rain, and their leaves contribute to the atmosphere by releasing oxygen, a by-product of photosynthesis. Many trees are planted for the shade their leafy branches provide, screening out the hot sunlight. Their woody trunks also provide valuable building materials.

Most of the trees that are grown for shade or wood belong to a single subclass, Hamamelididae. Its name comes from the scientific name of one of its members, the witch hazel (genus *Hamamelis*), whose bark yields a soothing lotion. (This tree's common name has nothing to do with witchcraft; it comes from an Old English word meaning "to yield"—the same root that gave us the modern word *weak*—and refers to the witch hazel's easily bent branches.) Orders in the witch hazel group include Hamamelidales (witch hazel and plane tree), Urticales (elm, nettle, and mulberry), Fagales (oaks, beech, birch, and hazel), and Juglandales (including walnut trees).

## FROM TINY ACORNS . . .

Oak trees are tall shade trees that bear nuts called acorns. (A **nut** is a fruit with a stony outer wall.) Oak trees grow rather slowly and don't produce acorns until they are at least twenty years old. But they live for a long time—200 to 400 years. Some species are evergreen; others lose their leaves each fall.

Acorns are a valuable source of food for the wildlife. Squirrels are known for stocking up on acorns so that they will have enough food to keep them going throughout the winter. Chipmunks store nuts in the burrows where they hibernate; they wake up now and then from their winter sleep to take a snack.

*Acorns of the scrub oak* (Quercus gambelii) *take two years to mature.*

Oak is a very important source of lumber. Oak wood is a popular choice for making furniture because it is heavy, hard, and sturdy, and it has an attractive grain.

## CRAZY ABOUT NUTS

Birches and beeches, members of the same order as the oaks, do not produce acorns, but beeches are well known for their sweet, edible nuts. Like acorns, beechnuts are a major source of food for squirrels, mice, and other wild animals.

Birch trees are easy to spot because their light-colored bark is usually split and peeling off in papery sheets. Native Americans used the bark to make birch-bark canoes. (The bark of the plane tree, or sycamore, also tends to peel, but it comes off in patches rather than large sheets.)

*The leaves of the paper birch* (Betula papyrifera) *turn a brilliant yellow in the fall.*

Walnut trees are valued both for their tasty nuts and for their beautiful wood. The coverings of the nuts have a shriveled appearance. Two popular walnut trees grown in the eastern part of the United States are the black walnut and the white walnut, or butternut tree. Black walnuts are used primarily for their attractive wood, although their nuts are edible. The butternut tree's wood is weaker and softer than that of the black walnut tree. Butternut trees have pointed leaves that are hairy and sticky.

Elms are large, beautiful shade trees commonly used in landscaping. Elm wood is difficult to split, which makes it a poor choice for burning in a campfire. The most popular elm grown in the United States is the American elm, also called the white elm. The American elm has branches that spread out like an umbrella.

## SYRUP AND SHADE

Maple trees are popular shade trees both in Europe and in North America. There are more than one hundred species, all in the order Sapindales in the rose group. One of them, the sugar maple, produces a sweet-smelling sap that is the source of the maple syrup we pour over pancakes. The maple leaf, with its easily recognized handlike shape, is the national symbol of Canada.

*Sugar maples* (Acer saccharum) *produce a sap that is used for maple sugar.*

How can you tell the difference between maple leaves and the similar-looking leaves of the sycamore, or plane tree? Both are hand-shaped leaves, usually with three or five separate "fingers," or lobes. But the outline of the maple leaf has deep indentations between the lobes, and the vein patterns are quite different. (Rows of parallel veins branch out from each main vein of the sycamore leaf.) The fruits are also very different. Sycamore fruits are brown balls, which break up into tiny fruitlets, each with a wisp of silky hairs that help to carry it off in the breeze.

Maple trees have fruits called keys. These fruits contain a pair of winged-shaped seeds. The seeds grow together so that they look like an airplane propeller.

*Seeds, or keys, of the red maple tree*
(Acer rubrum)

# 12

# THE YOUNGEST CLASS

An alternate name for the class Monocotyledones is Liliopsida. Botanists believe that members of the order Liliales—the lilies and their relatives—date back to the time of the dinosaurs and were ancestors of most of the present-day monocots.

## FIRST IN THEIR CLASS

The **lily** family (Liliaceae) includes beautiful bell-shaped flowers as well as popular foods. The white Easter lilies and the brightly colored day lilies and tiger lilies are popular members of this family. Their large, showy flowers have six petals that form a tube and then spread wide. The lilies' narrow, tapering leaves die down in the fall, but the plants are not dead. Enlarged buds, called **bulbs**, are waiting in the soil for warm weather to come again. With the spring warmth and rains, they send up green shoots that form leaves and flower stalks.

*Day lily* (Hemerocallis fulva)

Other flowers in the lily family include lilies of the valley, which form sprays of tiny, sweet-smelling bell-shaped flowers, and tulips, which have been bred to an incredible variety of colors and shapes. Daffodils and amaryllis belong to a related family in the lily order, and iris and crocus are members of still another family in the lily group. The family of true lilies includes some common foods: onions, garlic, and asparagus.

Onions are strong-smelling herbs used

to add flavor to soups, stews, casseroles, and other dishes. The onions themselves are bulbs, but the long green leaves may also be eaten and have a mild oniony flavor. When onions are peeled or sliced, they may bring tears to our eyes. That's because onions contain sulfur-rich oils that fill the air with vapors that irritate the eyes. Onions have long been known to have medical benefits. They have been used as treatments for colds, earaches, laryngitis, animal bites, powder burns, and warts. More recent studies suggest that they may help to protect against heart attacks by lowering blood pressure and cholesterol and making it less likely for clots to form inside blood vessels.

Garlic is similar to onions in that it has a powerful smell and has a strong taste as well. (Both onion and garlic belong to the same genus, *Allium*.) Garlic is often used to season foods. The garlic bulb comes in several parts, called cloves, which are covered by a papery film. Studies have shown that it may help to regulate blood pressure and cholesterol and has an antibiotic effect against various disease-causing bacteria.

Asparagus plants come out of the ground in little green shoots or stems. The shoots, also called spears, are the edible parts of the plant. Asparagus is a very nutritious vegetable containing a good amount of protein, vitamins, and minerals. After the spring harvesting season is over, the new asparagus stalks are allowed to grow, forming feathery leaflike branches 5 or 6 feet (1.5 or 1.8 meters) high and small greenish bell-shaped flowers, which later produce red berries. A type of asparagus people do not eat is the asparagus fern, which is usually used as a decoration in floral arrangements.

Tulips are popular flowers that grow from bulbs. The name *tulip* is a Turkish word for "turban"; the blossoms look like little turbans. People often plant tulip bulbs during the fall so that they can pop up in the spring. These beautiful bell-shaped flowers come in a wide variety of colors. Some tulips develop virus diseases that put streaks through their colors, but their health remains unaffected.

Daffodils originated in Europe, where they grow wild in the woods. In North America, the yellow trumpet-shaped flowers are commonly grown in gardens. Daffodils grow from individual bulbs and bloom in early spring. The bulbs are poisonous if eaten.

## SOME GRASSES ARE GOOD TO EAT

Everyone recognizes grass (family **Gramineae** in the order Poales) as that soft, green carpet we walk on at playgrounds, parks, and in many yards. It's everywhere! Grass covering not only beautifies the landscape, but it also protects fertile soil from eroding.

What we think of as the grass leaf is actually only part of it. The long, flat green "leaf" is actually a blade. The grass leaf also includes a tubular sheath that covers part of

Spaghetti and other kinds of pasta are made from durum wheat, a variety that developed in nature as a hybrid, or crossbreed, between two wild wheat grass species. People have been breeding wheat and other food plants for thousands of years, developing hardier plants that yield more nutritious crops. Now scientists are using micro-tools called gene guns to speed up the breeding process by transferring the genes for particular traits from one plant to another. They hope to produce new varieties of durum wheat that are resistant to plant diseases and give grain with more protein.

the blade. (Did you ever make a whistle out of a grass blade?) It's hard to imagine grass growing flowers, but it does. At least it would if the grass were never cut. But these flowers don't have any petals. They just form flower clusters that contain stamens and pistils from which seeds are formed. Grass flowers are pollinated by the wind, so they do not need showy petals or sweet smells to attract insect pollinators.

We seldom think of grass as something to eat, but there are numerous cereal grasses. These are grain grasses that produce seeds that can be eaten. They are among the most important and widespread crops in the world. They include wheat, rice, corn, and oats.

*Wheat* (Triticum aestivum) *is a cereal grain that yields a fine white flour. Wheat germ is the vitamin-rich wheat embryo separated in milling.*

More wheat is grown than any other crop, and millions of people all over the world eat the various foods made from it. Wheat kernels (seeds) are ground into flour and used to make bread, rolls, crackers, noodles, and breakfast cereals. Young wheat plants in the form of hay are also used to feed livestock. As a young plant, wheat looks like grass. It may grow up to 5 feet (1.5 meters) tall, and it turns golden brown as it ripens. The wheat kernels are located at the top center stem. The grains are white, red, or yellow when they are fully ripe.

Rice is also a very popular grain all over the world, especially in Asia. Many Asians eat rice three times a day—a total of about ½ to ⅔ of a pound (0.2 to 0.3 kilogram) of rice per person each day—whereas Americans eat about 9 pounds (4 kilograms) of rice each *year* per person. Rice is grown in areas that are warm and very wet, which would not be a favorable environment for other cereal grains.

Farmers must plant rice in fields where water is plentiful since rice needs a constant supply of water.

Corn, also known as maize, was first used by Native Americans about 10,000 years ago. Corn has become a valuable cereal grain, favored especially in the United States, which is the world's leading producer and exporter. Corn has a wide variety of uses. The corn kernels (seeds) can simply be cooked and eaten. They can also be used to make corn oil, corn syrup, and breakfast cereals. They can be ground to make flour (cornmeal). Large quantities of corn grain are used to feed livestock. Corn grains are also used in nonfood products, such as cosmetics, paper goods, drugs, paints, and textiles.

A corn plant has roots, a stalk, leaves, and flowering parts. Plants can grow anywhere from 3 to 20 feet (0.9 to 6 meters) high. At the top of the stalk is the flowering part, called the tassel, which contains the male reproductive cells (sperm). The female reproductive structures are located on the ears, in the middle of the stalk. Pollen from the tassels falls on the long, silky, threadlike stigmas that stick out of the ears. When the sperm and eggs unite inside the ear, the fertilized eggs develop into kernels on a cob. At least one pollen grain must land on each strand of "silk" for all the kernels on the cob to develop. The cob is covered and protected by leaves called husks.

Oats are another important cereal grain. In most parts of the world, oats are primarily used to feed livestock. In the United States, about 90 percent of the oats grown are used to feed farm animals. However, oat grains are also used in many food products such as oatmeal, cookies, and breakfast cereals. Oats have a greater nutritional value than any other cereal grain. They include a high-quality protein, and they provide a good source of vitamin $B_1$, called thiamine.

Bamboo is another member of the grass family. Sturdy branches grow up from underground stems called rhizomes, which help to bind the soil together. The bamboos of Malaysia grow 120 feet (36.5 meters) tall; their stems are valuable building materials. Hollowed-out bamboo stems are used as water pipes and as supports for beans and other climbing plants. If a field is not cared for regularly, bamboo runs wild and forms a forest. The bamboo stems contain silica and are very difficult to cut.

## JUICY FRUITS

Pineapple plants (order Bromeliales) are grown for their large, juicy fruit. The pineapple looks like a big pinecone, which is where its name originated. Worldwide, the most pineapple plants are grown in warm regions, such as Thailand, Brazil, and Indonesia. Hawaii dominates the pineapple production in the United States. The pineapple plant has large, sword-shaped leaves growing from a thick stem. There is also a group of smaller leaves coming out from the top of the pineapple, called the crown. Pineapple plants produce little flowers attached to a flower stalk located in the center, called the inflorescence. The **inflorescence** looks like a small, pink-red cone. The flowers then develop into little fruits. The fruits join together with the stalks they were attached to and form one massive fruit. The fruit itself is pale yellow, and the outer shell is yellowish brown when it's ripe.

Palms (order Palmales or Arecales) are a group of trees and shrubs with long, feathery leaves. They grow in warm climates. Coconut palms (*Cocos nucifera*) are among the oldest and most popular palms. Their tall trunks (stems) look slanted and then curve upward as they come to a crown of leaves. Coconut palms produce clusters of flowers throughout the year. It takes twelve months for each flower to open and the coconut to ripen. The 4- or 5-pound (about 2-kilogram) nut falls to the ground when it is fully ripened. This nut is actually one of the largest seeds produced from a plant. The inside of the coconut contains a clear jelly at first, which later liquefies into a clear "milk" that is a very refreshing drink in the tropics.

Coconut palms are believed to grow most successfully near the sea. South Sea islanders say that these trees grow well only when they can hear the sounds of the sea and the sounds of human voices. Coconuts have been carried by ocean waters to many tropical islands, where they have sprouted and multiplied. Coconut palms currently provide about a fifth of all the oils and fats in international trade.

Banana plants (family Musaceae) grow in hot, damp climates. They are often called trees, but they are not real trees because the stem is not made of wood. The stem consists of long leaves that grow very close together, one inside the other. Since the leaves stretch out in the air, the banana plant resembles a palm tree.

When the banana plant is ten months old, it grows a large flower at the end of a long, thick stalk. The flower has many purple leaves called **bracts**, which roll back, revealing clusters of small flowers. These flowers develop into small green bananas. Each cluster of flowers is called a hand and consists of ten to twenty bananas, which are known as fingers. As the bananas grow and become heavier, the stem droops down and the bananas begin to curve upward. For the best taste, bananas should be cut while they are still green and allowed to ripen afterward. (The bananas have usually started to turn yellow by the time they reach supermarkets.) Each banana plant produces only one bunch of bananas, which can weigh from 60 to 100 pounds (27 to 45 kilograms). When the banana plant finishes producing its fruit, the stem of the plant is chopped off and a new stem grows in its place, starting the cycle all over again.

Bananas are a popular fruit all over the world and currently the number-one fruit consumed in the United States. They are rich in vitamins A and C and in minerals such as potassium and phosphorus. In tropical societies, banana leaves are used to build roofs for houses and to make bags, baskets, and mats.

## THE ELITE ORDER

Orchids (order Orchidales) are exotic flowers known for their beauty and elegance. All orchids have three attractive petals, although they differ in color and shape. Orchids may take on interesting forms such as cups, scoops, or even trumpets. The largest of the three petals, the center, is called the lip or **labellum**, which secretes nectar. In one species, called the lady's slipper, the lip resembles a lady's shoe.

People usually think of orchids as tropical plants, but members of the family are found in numerous varied habitats around the world—even in the arctic climate of Alaska, Greenland, and Siberia. Many of the tropical orchids live high up in the air, on the limbs and bark of giant trees. They aren't parasites, though. Most orchids get their nourishment from the air, soil moisture, rain, and sunlight, using chlorophyll to make their own food by photosynthesis as other plants do. Long aerial roots stretch down to the soil and help to anchor them. Some species, such as the coral-roots, have no chlorophyll and feed on decayed matter in the soil. One tropical orchid, known as the vanilla orchid, produces vanilla beans. Vanilla flavoring is extracted from these beans and is used in many of our foods and beverages.

Orchid flowers have a special partnership with insects. Like other flowers, orchids rely on insects for pollination. But orchids are a bit more specialized. One specific species of insect or even one sex of that species is solely responsible for pollinating an orchid. Different species of insects are attracted to different types of orchids, depending on the fragrance and structure of the flower. Other flowers are not that discriminating.

*A hammer orchid has attracted a female thynnine wasp, which is the one insect species responsible for pollinating this kind of orchid.*

# IDENTIKEY

❧ ❧ ❧ ❧

**N**aturalists may use identification keys to help them in identifying plants and animals. For example, suppose it is summer, and you have just noticed a vine climbing up the side of your house. Here's an "identikey" that can help you determine what kind of plant it is.

**1.** Some or all of the stems are woody              **Go to step 2**

    None of the stems are woody              **Go to step 3**

**2.** Palmate leaves with a saw-toothed edge              **May be grapevine***

    Shiny compound leaves with 3 oval leaflets              **May be poison ivy!****

    Single oval leaves alternate along vine              **May be English ivy*****

**3.** Lobed, palmate leaves with smooth edge              **May be English ivy*****

    Groups of 3 or 5 oval leaves              **Go to step 4**

**4.** Leaves have wavy edge;
      trumpet-shaped blue, purple,
      or white flowers              **Probably morning glory**

    Groups of 3 leaflets; sweet-smelling red,
    yellow, white, pink, or purple flowers;
    long seed pods              **Probably bean*****

    Oval leaves alternate along vine              **May be English ivy*****

---

\* Was someone eating seeded grapes nearby?

\*\*Thoroughly wash skin and clothing that may have come into contact with plant. Use disposable gloves to remove vine.

\*\*\*Young leaves of English ivy are lobed and palmate; mature leaves are pointed ovals.

\*\*\*\*Is there a vegetable garden nearby? (Pod may have sprouted.)

**Note:** In the fall, English ivy has blue-black berries; poison ivy has clusters of ivory-white berries.

# A LITTLE LATIN HELPS

Knowing some basic Latin and Greek "building blocks" can help you guess the meaning of scientific terms.

| | | | |
|---|---|---|---|
| a- | without | -morph | form |
| amphi- | both | myc(o)- | fungus |
| antho- | flower | nona- | nine |
| bi- | two | oct(a)- | eight |
| bryo- | moss | -oid | like |
| carn(i)- | meat | omni- | everything |
| chlor(o)- | green | oo- | egg |
| coni- | cone | -ose | sugar molecule |
| cruci- | cross | ov(o)- | egg |
| cyano- | blue | para- | beside |
| deca- | ten | penta- | five |
| di- | two | -phil | loving |
| dodeca- | twelve | -phor(e) | carrier |
| domestica- | domestic, cultivated | photo- | light |
| endo- | inside | -phyll | leaf |
| epi- | upon, outer, besides | phyt(o)-, -phyt(e) | plant |
| eu- | true | -plast | granule, cell |
| exo- | outside | pro- | before |
| -fer | carrying | prot(o)- | first |
| fil- | thread | ptero- | fern |
| flor- | flower | rhiz(o)- | root |
| -form(es) | in the form of, resembling | sacchar(o)- | sugar |
| gam- | joined; pertaining to mating | sapro- | dead or decaying matter |
| | | sativa | common |
| hepta- | seven | -sperm | seed |
| herb(i)- | plant | stom- | opening |
| hetero- | different | tetra- | four |
| hexa- | six | tri- | three |
| homo- | same | vas(o)- | vessel, tube |
| maxi- | big | vir- | poison |
| mini- | little | -vore | eating |
| mon(o)- | one | | |

# GLOSSARY

**alternation of generations** — a process in which gametophytes, which reproduce sexually, alternate with sporophytes, which reproduce asexually.

**angiosperms** — flowering plants (division Anthophyta) in which the seeds are covered by a fruit.

**anther** — the pollen-producing part of a stamen.

**Anthophyta** — the division of flowering plants.

**areole** — a mound on a cactus stem, from which spines and flowers grow.

**bract** — a modified leaf, from which a flower arises.

**bryophytes** — mosses, liverworts, and hornworts; members of division Bryophyta.

**bulb** — an underground reproductive structure consisting of an enlarged bud.

**cactus** — a plant of family Cactaceae: desert plants that store water in thick stems and are protected by sharp spines.

**caffeine** — a chemical produced by coffee, tea, and cacao plants, which has a stimulant effect on humans.

**carnivorous** — meat-eating.

**cell** — the smallest functioning unit of life.

**cell membrane** — a thin, flexible covering surrounding a cell.

**cellulose** — a natural polymer made of glucose (sugar) units that forms the cell wall of plants.

**cell wall** — a tough, rigid outer covering surrounding a plant cell.

**chlorophyll** — a green substance found in plant cells that helps to capture sunlight energy.

**classification** — the process of dividing objects into related groups.

**club mosses** — vascular plants of division Lycophyta.

**composite** — a family of flowering plants (Compositae) with a flower head containing ray and disk flowers; include daisy, sunflower, and dandelion.

**cone** — the reproductive organ of conifers, in which seeds lie between protective scales.

**conifers** — cone-bearing gymnosperms (division Coniferophyta).

**cotyledon** — the first leaf of a seed plant.

**Cruciferae** — the mustard family, including vegetables such as cabbage, broccoli, cauliflower, and turnips.

**cycads** — a division (Cycadophyta) of gymnosperms.

**dicots** — flowering plants whose embryo has two cotyledons (class Dicotyledones).

**division** — in taxonomy, a major category in classification; applied to plants, bacteria, and sometimes to algae and fungi; corresponds to *phylum* in the animal kingdom.

**ferns** — plants of division Pterophyta, with long leaves (fronds) consisting of many leaflets.

**fertilization** — the joining of sperm and egg to form a new individual.

**filament** — the long stalk of a stamen.

**flower** — the reproductive organ of angiosperms; contains male and/or female parts.

**fronds** — the leaves of ferns, consisting of hundreds of tiny leaflets.

**fruit** — the ovule of a plant, containing ripe seeds, plus covering tissues.

**gametes** — sex cells (sperm and eggs).

**gametophyte** — a plant that produces sex cells.

**genus** — a group of rather closely related organisms.

**ginkgo** — the one remaining species of the gymnosperm division Ginkgophyta.

**gnetophytes** — gymnosperms of division Gnetophyta; include the genera *Ephedra*, *Gnetum*, and *Welwitschia*.

**Gramineae** — the family of grasses, including wheat, corn, rice, and other cereal grasses, as well as sugarcane and bamboo.

**gymnosperms** — seed-producing plants that do not have flowers; include conifers, cycads, ginkgo, and gnetophytes.

**horsetails** — vascular plants of division Sphenophyta.

**inflorescence** — a flower head.

**kingdom** — the largest group in the classification of living organisms.

**labellum** — the large central petal of an orchid, which secretes nectar.

**legumes** — plants of the pea family (Leguminosae), which bear fruits in the form of pods; form nodules on the roots, which provide shelter for nitrogen-fixing bacteria; include peas, beans, peanuts, alfalfa, and clover.

**lily** — a monocot flowering plant believed to be the ancestor of present-day monocots.

**liverworts** — bryophytes of class Hepaticopsida, which are small and have no vascular system.

**magnolia** — a dicot flowering plant believed to be the most like the first angiosperms.

**monocots** — flowering plants whose embryo has only one cotyledon (class Monocotyledones).

**mosses** — bryophytes of class Muscopsida, which are small and have no vascular system.

**nightshade** — a family of plants (Solanaceae) including belladona, tobacco, tomato, potato, eggplant, and pepper.

**nut** — a fruit with a stony outer wall.

**opium** — a drug produced by the opium poppy (*Papaver somniferum*) and used to manufacture morphine and heroin.

**ovary** — the part of the pistil in which eggs are produced.

**ovule** — structure containing the female sex cell (egg) of an angiosperm.

**photosynthesis** — the conversion of carbon dioxide and water to sugars and starches, using the energy from sunlight.

**pistil** — a female part of a flower, in which eggs are produced.

**Plantae** — the plant kingdom.

**pollen** — powdery substance containing the male sex cells (sperm) of an angiosperm.

**pollination** — the transfer of pollen from an anther to a stigma (of the same or another flower).

**pterophytes** — ferns; members of division Pterophyta.

**resin** — a sticky substance secreted by conifers.

**rhizoid** — a rootlike structure; found in bryophytes.

**Rosaceae** — the rose family, which also includes apples, cherries, plums, peaches, pears, almonds, and strawberries.

**sori** — clusters of sporangia on undersides of fern fronds.

**species** — a group of very closely related organisms, each able to breed with others in the group.

**sporangia** — spore-producing structures in ferns.

**spore** — a single cell that can grow into a plant.

**sporophyte** — a plant that produces spores.

**stamen** — a male part of a flower, in which pollen is produced.

**stigma** — the top of the pistil, on which pollen grains land.

**stomates** — openings on the underside of plant leaves, used for respiration.

**strobilus** — the cone (reproductive organ) of cycads.

**taproot** — a single broad root.

**taxonomy** — the science of classifying or arranging living things into groups based on the characteristics they share.

**tuber** — portion of a stem enlarged and modified to store starch and other nutrients.

**vascular system** — an arrangement of tubes, running from plant roots through the stems to the leaves, that conduct water and food materials.

**veins** — the conducting tubes in a leaf; they form characteristic patterns that help in identifying plants.

**whisk ferns** — vascular plants of division Psilophyta.

# INDEX